SALES SELF-SABOTAGE
Overcoming Personality Barriers to Achievement

By Lane A Stokes L.P.C.

ISBN: 1489500103
ISBN-13: 9781489500106

Preface

If you as a salesperson feel that something is holding you back from making a lot more sales, then this book is for you.

If you as a sales manager cannot understand why you cannot train and motivate your agents to achieve more sales, then this book is for you.

If you as the spouse of a salesperson cannot understand how your other half can work so long and hard to produce so little income, then this book is for you.

If you have never understood why 80% of the salespersons can only sell 20% of the goods and services while the 20% sell 80%, then this book is for you.

If you want to know how I have learned to change the 80% Personality to the upper 20% Personality, then this book is for you.

Actually, SALES SELF-SABOTAGE is about achievement and could apply to anybody desiring to achieve more in any endeavor such as business, relationships, winning golf tournaments, breaking world's records in sports, and so forth. The book targets salespersons because in our 2013 economy the scarcity of jobs has driven millions into sales. The personality barriers that seem not to affect salaried individuals suddenly become huge when money must be earned on a day-to-day basis as in straight-commission selling. It is the Purpose of this book to identify the many unconscious personality barriers that cause self-sabotage to achievement, and to describe methods being used to change the 80% Personality to the upper 20% Personality, by removing those barriers in a relatively short amount of time.

Although this book can be read in one sitting, you will find it an invaluable Handbook for identifying symptoms of the various personality barriers that prevent high achievement.

Acknowledgements

I dedicate this book to my wife Nancy whose love, patience, and wisdom has made it possible.

I acknowledge all those who have influenced my life from birth till now, but especially recently as described below.

My brother Richard Stokes who spent many hours sharing his wisdom how to more effectively communicate my thoughts in letters, advertisements and seminars.

To David Wiley who was the first sales manager of my experience open to the idea that 80% of salespersons achieved so little because of personality barriers instead of laziness. He also introduced me to David Gore, and continues to encourage my research and efforts in changing the 80% Personalities into the upper 20%.

To David Gore, Agency Manager of Insphere Insurance Solutions in Atlanta, who invited me to present my ideas to his sales agents, and supported me in developing a group seminar approach for changing the 80% Personality into the upper 20% Personality.

To Alan Harrell, Belinda Reed, Joanna Scott and McKinley Stinson who worked with me during the three months it took to develop three different seminars, by their participation, inspiration and sharing of ideas.

To Chuck Russell, CEO of Best Work Data, LLC who encouraged me to write this book.

To Hal Coleman who helped me state with clarity exactly what I do.

Table of Contents

Introduction

The Sales Paradigm is changing. A discovery has been made that is now transforming the personality of the 80% of salespersons into that of the upper 20% of high achievers. Those who did not have a chance to "choose" developing the special 20% Personality during the first year of life, can now choose at any age. It is the Purpose of this book to identify the many unconscious personality barriers that cause self-sabotage of achievement, and to describe methods being used to change the 80% Personality to the upper 20% Personality by removing those barriers in a relatively short amount of time.

Unaware that change is possible, the average salesperson continues to give the same old excuses for frittering away yet another day, when he or she could be making appointments and calling on prospective clients. Never has the average salesperson or his or her predecessors ever pondered, "I wonder what unconscious personality trait is sabotaging me today?" It won't be long before this will be his or her first query when unable to make the hoped for sales.

Since 1907 when Pareto's Principle of the 20%/80% became popular, and the Sales Industry seized it as the statistic best explaining why so few salespersons succeeded, it has been agreed upon by the sales community that 80% do indeed sell only 20% of the goods and services. Why, in all those years with progressively better sales training and technology has that statistic remained true? It is because of self-sabotage caused by old attitudes, beliefs and behaviors that still control the personality of the 80% from the unconscious mind. More specifically, it is the effects of what this author calls Personality Traits and Personality Drivers. These personality Traits and Drivers are made worse by prevailing attitudes and beliefs of sales managers, sales trainers, sales coaches and self-help books, seminars and motivational materials purporting the traditional ideals. These ideals are yet to be informed by those of us who have sat with hundreds of clients, and noted the destruction to personal and business relationships by these ingrained attitudes and beliefs.

How to get what you want is no longer a mystery or "hocus-pocus". It is the simple science of identifying the unconscious personality traits and drivers in you that hold you back from attaining your goals, and then overcoming or changing those traits or drivers.

Since 1979, many people have had their personalities transformed by the same principles now being focused exclusively on changing personalities of salespersons for greater productivity. Soon companies will enjoy the retention of all their sales agents without the expensive re-hiring processes, which have long been the norm. Instead of losing agents, then, companies will grow larger, with every agent producing at top levels of achievement, gaining a larger market share, and towering over their competitors.

Disclaimer: Although this author is sensitive to gender issues, to make reading this book easier, the standard "he" or "him" will be used instead of "he or she" and so forth.

Section I
20% And 80% Personalities

Vilfredo Pareto, an Italian economist observed in 1906 that 80% of the land in Italy was owned by 20% of the population and discovered that 20% of the pea pods produced 80% of the peas. From that day to this, Pareto's Principle has been used to explain many things, one of which is why 20% of the salespersons sell 80% of the goods and services, while the other 80% sell only 20%. That's unfortunate, because companies now depend on the top 20% to keep the doors open and salaries paid, while expecting very little from the other 80%. It's also sad because the 80% want to earn the same money as the 20% and enjoy a richer lifestyle for their family. One intention of this book is to change the prevailing attitudes regarding the 80%/20% rule by using valuable information discovered over many decades of research. After finishing this book, the reader will have a better understanding of how to change from an 80% personality to one of the 20%.

Chapter 1
The 20% Personality

Affectionately, I refer to the 20% as little wind-up toys—you wind 'em up and away they go. Their minds are so clear, so focused as they ignore anything that gets in the way of reaching the goal of whatever they desire. They quickly rise to the top of whatever industry they choose, becoming generals in the military, The President in politics, chief of staff of hospitals, bishop, rabbi, pope, gold medalists, CEO's of companies and the list goes on. In sales, they become Salesperson of the Month, then Salesperson of the Year and rise quickly to the top of their company. How do they do it? Are they born with this talent? Almost. Many mental health professionals now believe that perhaps the baby is born with a genetic predisposition toward development of that 20% personality type.

During that first year of life, the infant's first impression is that his body and that of his mother are the same. It is during this phase that the infant believes or has a sense that he is omnipotent because what he thinks, he gets. For example, he thinks, "I am hungry", and the mother feeds him. Toward the end of those first 12 months his eyes develop, and he realizes that his body is not the same as the mother's, and he also observes that she does not always bring the milk, no matter how much he thinks he wants it. Therefore, he realizes on some level that he is not omnipotent, and at some unconscious level, goes through a brief period of depression while accepting the belief that life will be more difficult that first thought. He will have to figure out ways to get what he wants through trial and error. There will be some successes and some failures. Who knows what a baby thinks, but the theory plays out true in later years. The 80% do have to settle for a life of struggle. What about the 20%? For some reason nobody yet understands, the 20% never accept the belief that they are not omnipotent even though they do recognize the separateness of the bodies. From infancy to old age they live with the expectation of getting everything they desire, and they do, for the most part. This personality works wonderfully in sales.

I once had a sales manager who would come into the office in the morning, pick up the phone book, turn his head away and put his finger down on a name. Then he would call that number, set an appointment with that person for the same night and come in the next morning with a signed contract. He would say to us, "If I can do it, you can do it." What he didn't realize is that the great majority of sales agents are not like him. The incorrect beliefs most sales managers have are the main reasons the 80% remain stuck where they are. The good news is that if a manager has the right set of tools, he can help his salespeople to become the sales team of his dreams.

Chapter 2
The 80% Personality

My research has taught me that the 20% have at least 60 strong personality traits that push them toward achievement, while the 80% may have these same traits, but in a weaker form. Self-esteem and self-confidence are always weak in the 80%. No captivating presence or the ability to resonate with customers exists. There is not much physical energy and there appears to be an almost total lack of desire. The 80% can, however, possess over 200 possibly significant and debilitating unconscious personality components that force the person into self-sabotage, low achievement and failure. It is no wonder that they seldom have much success in sales. The more people they see, the more discouraged they become. They don't realize that they are not even connecting with prospective clients. While the 20% call 5 people to set one appointment and close 9 of 10 sales, the 80% may call 50 to just set one appointment, and are lucky if they close one of six. Why do they even try? An even more interesting question is, "Why do companies continue wasting huge sums of money hiring people from whom they expect so little?"

Why do the 80% try to sell? They need money to pay their bills. They believe that they have the personality for selling. They want a lot of money and believe that selling is the only way to get it. They want to be their own bosses, set their own schedules and have free time—and this is where the problems arise. In a salaried job, we seldom notice personality barriers, but in sales those barriers make themselves apparent. What ends up happening in most cases is that the 80% make less money selling in that first year because of the lag time of training, learning products and learning how to sell. By the second year they realize that something is still holding them back although they cannot imagine what it is. The sales manager keeps telling them to schedule their time more wisely and see more people, but for reasons beyond their control the 80% continue to procrastinate, allow their customers to procrastinate, and don't make much money. I'm writing this book to speak to those who make so little for the energy expended worrying about why they aren't doing well. In answer to the question of why the 80% try to sell, they have to do something and this is what they choose. The 80% salespersons may never understand why they fail until they understand what I call "personality drivers."

Why do companies continue to hire the 80% when they have such low expectations of those people? First, it is because the hiring managers don't know how to scientifically define the 80% and 20% personalities or how to spot self-sabotaging traits. Second, they need replacements for the other 80% who have gotten fired or just never came back from lunch one day. The biggest myth is that everybody has an equal opportunity and equal abilities for getting to the Winner's Circle, so they hire those they think have the best personality and will work the hardest. The idea that anybody can become a top salesperson probably comes from the conditioned belief that some succeed and therefore so can the rest. I say "conditioned" because it's like the man who fishes in a trout stream and catches a whopper one day. For the next 20 years he continues to fish there even though he never catches another fish of any size. That's a type of conditioning as defined by the psychologists. The fact is that few of the 80% even get to the *lower* rungs of the upper 20% without specialized help.

In 1979, a gifted psychologist helped me recognize many of my personality traits that were holding me back, not only in my career, but also in my life. Thus began a life long journey, not only to improve my own abilities, but to help others overcome the same barriers I had, and enjoy a new level of success. This book will give you more insight into how I made those changes. We begin with a discussion of personality traits and drivers.

Section II
Personality Traits And Drivers

The terms Personality Traits and Personality Drivers are unique to me in the way that I define them. A Personality Trait for the purposes of this book is NOT "a distinguishing characteristic or quality of one's personal nature" as the dictionary would insist, but rather a positive or negative force that controls a person's behavior from the unconscious mind. I speak of the unconscious mind rather than the more popular subconscious mind because we clearly have communication with the subconscious mind. For instance, you can ask your subconscious mind to retrieve from your memory the name of a person you cannot remember at the present time, and after awhile the name may come into your conscious mind. But you cannot speak to your unconscious mind without knowing how, through specialized training.

As a Senior Mental Health Clinician I discovered "pieces" of mental illnesses that I referred to as "traits". I called them "traits" because those who assembled the DSM, the psychiatric Bible of Mental Illnesses, did not define them as mental illnesses. Even though these traits were not defined as mental illnesses, they had the same power of control over the thoughts and behaviors of their hosts, as would the full-blown illness.

After a short while I began using the word "trait" to describe a "piece" of the personality having less power than a "driver", which I define as a stronger type of trait. One such piece of a greater power that I called a driver was of the Borderline Personality Disorder. That driver is the "The Pleaser Personality". We will study more about this fascinating driver in a later chapter. For now, I want to help you understand the less powerful "traits" that were developed earlier in life, but that still control your thoughts and behaviors as you seek to become a more successful salesperson. But remember, just because I refer to them as less powerful does not mean that any one of them could not control your attitudes, beliefs and behaviors so as to cause self-sabotage. If a trait is so powerful as to cause self-sabotage of your selling ability, then think how much more powerful a driver could be.

One reason the Sales Industry has not been able to change the 20/80 rule is because of the "Slot Machine Effect", which is a form of conditioning. Every once in a while an agent will overcome a minor trait and have the normal burst of energy that results. One normal burst of energy could cause a tripling of sales for a week or two. Since traits can occur in patterns of 20 or more, it is not unusual for the agent to over-come another minor trait in the same pattern and experience another temporary boost. This conditioning effect thus causes the agent to believe that he can overcome any barriers to success. The fact is that even though they do overcome two or three minor traits in a pattern, most agents never overcome another one in that pattern, so the pat-tern persists. If the pattern produces low self-esteem, for instance, that agent will continue having low self-esteem that could prevent any significant success in his or her career. The new minor traits he over-comes in the future will only be a minor trait of another pattern. It is a cruel illusion that keeps the Sales Industry teaching the myth that all an agent has to do is work harder, and focus on overcoming all barriers, and they will.

In changing the 80% Personality to the 20%, I constantly run up against a common problem when a client experiences the overcoming of one trait. When the temporary boost causes him to be covered up with appointments, he incorrectly believes that weekly sessions are no longer needed. Getting only 1/10th of 1% of the 100% I have to offer, the agent will leave only to lose momentum and not return due to embarrassment or pride for being wrong. It takes a lifetime to develop the personality traits and drivers that prevent achievement, and the only way to change to the upper 20% Personality is by overcoming all those traits and drivers. One must not be fooled by the boost in sales that comes from one barrier being overcome, but must stay the course until all are overcome. Agents who drop out of the process never think in terms of "if I have tripled my appointments by getting 1/10 of 1% of the 100% available, what would happen to my sales if I gained 100%?"

When individuals do stay with the process and allow me to help them overcome all the traits in a pattern, the energy released normally causes a great increase in achievement of a permanent nature. Keep in mind, then, that because drivers are far more powerful than traits, to allow yourself to overcome a driver most often causes the doubling of one's income on a permanent basis. That's when we can begin building a basis for true wealth by overcoming all the remaining drivers and traits. *Prompting the Unconscious Mind* is the primary tool for overcoming all the traits in a pattern. You will learn about "Prompting" in Section III.

In the beginning of each chapter pertaining to Traits and Drivers I will state the main "symptoms" or characteristics so that you may discover which are controlling you.

Chapter 3

Unconscious Personality Traits

A Few of the Main symptoms or characteristics:
- **Low Self-Esteem**
- **Low Self-Confidence**
- **Procrastination**
- **Lack of Organization**
- **Easy Discouragement**
- **Heightened Emotions**
- **Lack of Connection with prospective client**
- **Anger, Frustration, and Hopelessness**

One person does not necessarily have all of the above symptoms, but those of the 80% normally have more than one. The 20% seldom have any of these.

Growing to maturity means, in part, taking control of one's life by being responsible for one's actions. It is a struggle to leave dependency to become our own persons, to be in control, and to be self-sufficient. We have to choose our own values, leaving our parents in order to move on, adding or subtracting from those values of our parents. We get nervous when we think that we still don't have it all together by the time we are twenty-one. Sometimes we become defensive when our peers seem to have achieved much more than we have. Therefore, when a professional comes along and says that you have dozens of personality traits that are causing self-sabotage of your life and sales career, it is normal to resist with all your might. Yet, in your resistance you must pay attention to the fact that your life isn't working perfectly and you are not getting all that you want. People like Adam Phillips become valuable to you by sharing their insights into personality development. Phillips wrote in his article *The Magical Act of a Desperate Person*, "No one recovers from the sadomasochism of their childhood"...There is something intrinsically and unavoidably humiliating about being a child."

It is a fact that nobody gets out of childhood unscathed, and many of the attitudes and beliefs we form before the age of five are never overcome in an entire lifetime. The childhood hope or dream of being a perfect person is a myth with which we all must come to terms. Is there something wrong with you? For the purposes of this book—no, because this book deals with decisions you made to survive situations into which you were thrust, mostly beyond your control. The fact that you are reading this book may be your first step in the right direction for correcting some of the wrong decisions you made earlier in life. The good news is, you can overcome your obstacles and achieve the goals you set for yourself.

What could some of these obstacles be? Surely you have not lived long enough by age 21 to have that many, you think. But...you actually do have attitudes and beliefs you created to protect yourself and get what you wanted in various situations in which you found yourself, from birth to the age you are now. How many situations were you thrust into and how many little "laws" did you make to protect your well being, or to get what you wanted or needed? Let's look at three of these below.

1.) Surely you cannot remember when you were 6 months old and wanted milk, but if you were one of those smart kids, you quickly discovered that by crying twice as loudly, Mother brought the milk twice as fast. At that point you had created two new beliefs: cry loud and the milk comes, or cry louder and the milk comes faster. Then Mother catches on and won't bring it at all until you have calmed down. What happened to those two beliefs? They didn't evaporate because you no longer found them useful; they sank into your unconscious mind where they continued to wait for an opportunity to be useful again. Then, that time came when you were two and threw a temper tantrum. You shouldn't be able to remember that either because it was before the age of 5, but your parents might. When being loud didn't work, you might have tried being louder. Maybe that worked or maybe you got punished. Again, as you outgrew the need for tantrums, the beliefs sank back into your unconscious mind until your raging hormones at age 15 reminded you of the power of "loud" and "louder", which, seemed to work well in getting your way with your be-frazzled mother. What is "loud and louder"? It is an unconscious personality trait that is waiting to be useful again some day. You may have a hard time believing that you made a conscious decision to use it to get what you wanted during a particular situation of your life at age 6 months, but you did at the sensory level, if none other. Let's look at one for which you can take responsibility.

2.) You were 14 when, at the urging of an older sibling you joined the church basketball team. Unlike him, who was the team favorite in high school, you warmed the bench more than you played. It was embarrassing to sit on that bench while your friends played and so you always defended your honor when teased about "warming the bench". You tried to make yourself look good, especially to the girls, by saying that you were not as old and therefore didn't have their skills-- but you knew better. You knew that you weren't very enthusiastic and didn't come to all the practice sessions, that you didn't deserve to play as much as the others. Inside, your lack of interest and lack of self-discipline chopped away at your ego and self-esteem. Twenty years later, as a salesperson, those attitudes you formed from those debilitating beliefs about you are now a trait, controlling your thoughts and behaviors from your unconscious mind. When needing to pick up the phone and call leads, you do not, because you don't believe that you deserve as much as the better salespersons—"the players"—and you think of yourself as not very enthusiastic or self-disciplined—just as you did then when warming the bench. Is there something wrong with you? No. You were exhibiting the best behavior you could have in that situation 20 years ago, just as if it were today. The reason you feel the same way as you did then is because there is still a "charge" on that memory. A charge is one of the reasons why we remember things. A charge is an unresolved emotion. Living in your unconscious mind are millions of memories that do not have charges attached to them and therefore cannot be remembered by the conscious mind. You are doing nothing wrong. This is why I say that there is nothing wrong with you even if you have dozens of traits. You have those traits because you made the best decision at that time to protect yourself when involuntarily thrust into a new situation. Recognizing what you are doing in the present tense, you can change your behavior displayed

20 years ago, unless a Driver is controlling your behavior. Sometimes you can discharge the emotion by simply observing what you are doing and not liking the effect, but often it will take a role-play to take away the charge. If the larger Driver is controlling you, however, you may not be able to remove the charge and will continue to be controlled by the trait. Then it would be time to contact a sales coach like myself to work with you to disable that driver. Let's look at another example just to make sure you understand.

3.) At age 16 you were looking at a boy you **knew** that you were in love with, even though he didn't know it yet. He was alone on the steps outside the school and you began walking his way without a clue as to how you would connect with him. From out of nowhere came MaryAnn, cheerleader and Homecoming Queen. You turned back nearly in tears. Why would he want you when he could have her? At that point you made a little law stating that no boy would ever want you because you didn't have her looks, her charm, or her giggly personality. That law soon became an unconscious personality trait that controlled you every time you even thought about boys or dating. Today you might be a Realtor at an open house with two other agents, one a handsome man and the other what you would consider a beautiful woman. What happens when a prospective buyer comes in? You wither. Is there something wrong with you? No. At age 16 you made the best decision you could as how best to protect your budding self. Today, you are still being controlled by those feelings of embarrassment and fear. Unless you have a personality driver somehow involved with those feelings of embarrassment and fear, you can change the way you think because you now recognize what has been controlling you. If you cannot make that change, then a driver with more power than the trait is controlling you and it is time to contact a sales coach like me to overcome that driver. These three examples show the power of traits that will continue to control you from your unconscious mind until you recognize them emotionally and seek a way to change your behavior. In all three cases you must consciously recognize or identify the effect and make a conscious effort to change your belief and behavior.

In summary of these three situations it is easy to understand how we all form countless attitudes and beliefs to protect us, and to get what we want or need. When we each have outgrown the need for those beliefs, or no longer need them, they sink into the unconscious mind where they continue to serve you when you need them—and they continue to control you.

Let's say that you have only 25 attitudes and beliefs from old situations that stop you today from having what you want. As I stated in the last two examples, you must first recognize the attitude or trait in order to change it. It's not enough to read about it in a book or have somebody tell you that people have these traits; you must recognize them in yourself by your own experience of self-discovery. As any psychiatrist, psychologist or licensed counselor will tell you, counseling tends to be a slow process because the professional cannot tell you what is bothering you. He or she must lead you to self-discovery. That can take a long, long time. Tackling one issue at a time, the client works consciously through to completion. How many years would it take for you to work through all those issues, one at a time—or should I say, how many lifetimes? This is why 80% of the salespersons never, ever sell more than 20%. Discouraged? Hopeless? Not at all. You are probably just where you need to be in order to get help…help that can change your life. Let's imagine that you and I are working together.

I prompt your unconscious mind to identify every personality trait that is holding you back and cause your unconscious mind to overcome every barrier all at the same time. This may take months, but certainly does not need to take years or lifetimes. If you were using only your conscious mind, you could only overcome one trait at a time and therefore would have to be "conscious" of every trait that you were to overcome. At the same time, I am prompting your unconscious mind to build more traits of strength that can cause a higher degree of achievement. The unconscious mind is not limited in the number of traits it can deal with at the same time, whereas the conscious mind can focus on only one at a time.

Although the stated purpose of this book is not a "How-to" or "Self-Help", many who read it will certainly try to use it in that way. From birth we all develop an attitude that we must "do it ourselves" without help from others. While this is a normal part of development toward maturity, it can also be pure stubbornness and work toward one's disadvantage. Licensed counselors study for years to understand how the personality works and then spend years with one patient trying to unlock a mental illness. For you to believe that you don't need professional help in overcoming "pieces" of mental illnesses ingrained in you over a lifetime is really rather arrogant, don't you think? While I cannot teach you in this book how to fully overcome a pattern of traits and certainly not a driver, I can help you notice how traits and drivers control you. At the end of each chapter, I can make you aware of the tendencies of your behavior as applicable to Drivers. The purpose of this book as stated is to provide information to change traditional and prevailing attitudes toward the 80% and 20% personalities and to show methods by which these personalities are already being changed. Below, you will find help for identifying some of your traits.

Self-Help and How-To

In this book, only three examples of traits are provided. Each person has the possibility of over 200 traits, so describing them in the same detail as the drivers are described would cause the book to have too many pages. The best way for you to discover some of your own traits without seeking professional help is to list all attitudes, beliefs and behaviors that you think prevent sales. Some of these might be low self-esteem, low self-confidence, procrastination, wasting time, poor organization, and fear. Pick one and try to overcome it by yourself. Many salespersons choose "procrastination". Because your conscious mind will only be able to focus on one trait at a time, your other traits may continue causing low productivity while you are trying to overcome procrastination. Go to the library. Countless books have been written on the subject and many more are being published. Try out other's ideas for ways to stop procrastinating.

It can be difficult to identify a pattern that may exist in procrastination. You may overcome two or three traits and have a temporary boost in sales. But other pieces of the procrastination puzzle may cause the procrastination to return once the temporary boost has ended. *Prompting the Unconscious Mind* in Section III will provide more help with the patterns. It is beyond the scope of this book to help the reader discover the deeper relationships of your traits to anger, shame, guilt and other emotions that cause self-sabotage. The *One Assessment* begins the process of overcoming those.

We will now move to a discussion of Drivers.

Chapter 4
The Caretaker
Personality Driver

Main Characteristics:
- **You fail to set an appointment during a call or fail to make a sale during an appointment but say to yourself, "At least I made her feel better about losing her husband."**
- **You teach the prospective client everything there is to know about your product or service without getting the sale, paving the way for a competitor to step right in and close the sale later.**

Taking care of clients is good; being a Caretaker Personality is not. We take care of our clients by selling them what is best for them, not by being pretend-counselors or ministers.

The Caretaker Personality is an expression of the purpose of one's life to get acknowledgement. The driver part of this personality causes us to want to feel important and to receive praise and acknowledgement. Since we all like feeling important and appreciated, the driver is not easy to overcome. It must be coaxed out of a person over time to make a distinction between the work of selling and the responsibility of shouldering the responsibility of being the caretaker of the client's feelings. The successful separation or distinction, then, allows the person to no longer be a caretaker when selling, while continuing that role of caretaker in his personal life.

The Caretaker is a driver. Let's review the hierarchy of traits and drivers. One trait is not as powerful as one driver in controlling our attitudes, beliefs and behaviors. But one trait can control your attitudes, beliefs and behaviors. A pattern of traits is not as powerful as one driver. In this book, the drivers are listed from weakest in power to greatest in power. "The Caretaker Driver" is the weakest and the "I Will Not" is the strongest. The six drivers listed are not all of them. What makes both traits and drivers difficult to overcome are the emotions that accompany them. For the Caretaker Driver, the key emotion is shame.

It is not the scope of this book to explain how emotions affect traits and drivers. This is why we urge our readers to simply become aware of the tendencies that accompany the drivers in hopes of being more successful in getting appointments and closing more sales. The Caretaker Personality, like all drivers, is quite complicated. Some with this driver feel ashamed of being a caretaker, and deep down wish that they were not caretakers. Again, this is why coaxing is the effective solution. Nobody can just say, "Get over it!" and cause the person to abstain from being a caretaker.

Anytime you feel ashamed or embarrassed about something, you can be sure that shame is involved in the makeup of that feeling. Most people use Guilt and Shame interchangeably because they do not know the difference. A person feels guilty when he has not done something. But, one feels shame when he believes that there is something actually wrong with the self. Those with shame will avoid professional help even to the destruction of self because of the fear of embarrassment. Without professional help, the person will most likely never get past that shame. Shame goes away when one talks about the event that caused it. People won't talk to family or friends about such an event. Talking to a professional that you don't see in your everyday life is different. Once you talk about the details, the feelings of embarrassment most often lessen or evaporate, and the healing process begins. It is the source of the feeling of embarrassment and humiliation that must be coaxed out of a person over time. Just knowing that you have the feeling does not make it go away. While we're on the subject of shame let's talk about traditional sales meetings and motivation measures.

When all the salespersons are present in a "Friday Cool-Down" session, usually mandatory by sales management, shame increases in the 80%. In many cases, agents are required to go to the chalkboard in front of the others and write their numbers for the week. Those whose numbers are lowest are shamed, which means that every person except the top salesperson gets shamed and feels less worthy to be a member of the sales team and sometimes of the human race. This practice is meant to be a motivation to cause the underlings to work harder to compete, but over time the erosion of the self-esteem undermines a person's ability to compete or do better. Only the upper 20% are motivated by shaming because it may be the only emotion that has traditionally been effective in overcoming the inertia of those top salespersons. They don't seem to mind feeling the shame for a few moments, because to them, it's just part of the game. For the 80% personality, the feeling deepens and lasts forever. One of these days some very smart sales manager is going to read a book about shame and stop using that method of so-called "motivation". He or she will then be able to watch the company productivity numbers soar.

Self-Help and How-To

If you have this driver, you will need to watch for your tendencies…
- To act like a counselor to your client rather than asking for an appointment or closing the sale.
- To educate the prospect or client rather than obtain an appointment or close the sale.
- To feel that you are not succeeding because there is something intrinsically wrong with you.

By becoming aware of your tendencies, you might be able to obtain more appointments and close more sales.

The next strongest Driver is the Pleaser Personality

Chapter 5

The Pleaser Personality Driver

Main Characteristics:

- **You waste a lot of energy making sure that the prospective customer likes you and making sure that he or she knows that you like him.**
- **Until mutual admiration is established it is virtually impossible for you to make the sale.**
- **If he says that the lack of money is preventing his buying the product, you will most likely agree not to sell it because you don't want to risk disapproval.**
- **You'd rather be liked than prosperous.**
- **You cannot risk losing the approval of someone who has stroked your self-worth.**

In the introduction of Traits and Drivers, I began by talking about a "piece" of the Borderline Personality Disorder. This "piece" of that particular mental illness is used to illustrate the power of control of a driver over one's thoughts and behaviors. The Pleaser Personality is one of the Drivers derived from the Borderline Personality Disorder. People tend to get confused with this term of "pleaser personality" because we like to please others when we can, especially in selling because our customers respond well to this attitude. But my use of The Pleaser Personality is not about pleasing clients in a constructive or positive way. When I hire salespersons for companies I screen out those having this pleaser personality, so understand the fact that when I use the term it has nothing to do with your attempting to help your customers. It is all about how the trait in you stops you from selling. This Driver called the Pleaser Personality comes to the child by the necessity to respond to an authority figure like a parent, in a pathological or unhealthy way. If you should have this Driver, then you will most likely respond to your customer as if this person is an authority figure instead of an equal. Such a response by you will allow him or her to control the sales appointment, which most likely would end with no contract.

The power of this pleaser personality driver comes from the psychological conditioning found in the Borderline Personality Disorder. Again, we are talking about a "piece" of the disorder, so that having the driver does not mean that you have the disorder. This explanation is being given for you to simply understand the power of the driver over your behavior. Perhaps you remember from your school years the experiments done with rats. The rat in a cage stepped on a bar to cause a peanut to fall out so that the rat could eat it. Then, at some point when the rat stepped on the bar, an electrical shock was applied. After that, the rat no longer would step on the bar to get the peanut. In the Borderline Personality Disorder, the mother creates this disorder in the child by certain conditioning to control the behavior of the child. What makes the disorder—and subsequently the "piece" or driver of this disorder—so powerful is that it is linked to the survival mechanism of the individual. The mother conditions the child to obey by withholding milk, for example, in infancy. The infant obeys because of his sense of death if he does not get the milk. The conditioning in infancy is so strong that for the rest of that child's life, disobedience to the mother causes a horrible fear response. Although the child does not remember the milk being withheld in infancy, he responds with the same fear of dying if he disobeys. As an adult, he responds with that same fear of dying every time he disobeys his mother. By understanding this conditioning, it becomes easier to comprehend how even a "piece" of this disorder could be so strong in controlling behavior. The human need to please a client, even to the point of losing the sale, is controlled by an inner impulse over which you have no control. Professional help becomes invaluable at this point. Many of the 80% personality have this driver and it is one reason that the 80% continue to sell only 20% of the goods and services.

Salespeople having this "piece" or "driver" will have great difficulty in connecting with sales prospects because of the confusion of wondering what he or she must do to please the prospect in order to get the appointment or the sale. Until now, those with the pleaser personality have simply washed out of sales or have been fired. The good news is that now there are some ways that may help you overcome that driver so that you can succeed in sales.

Self-Help and How-To

While selling, you must become aware of your tendency...

- To spend a lot of time "warming up" the prospective client before getting to the subject at hand.
- To treat the opinion of your prospect or client as more important than your own.
- To want to agree with everything your prospect or client says.
- To allow your prospect or client to control the sales meeting.
- To feel sorry for a customer who says that the lack of money is the reason for not buying.

As with the all the drivers, you are not trained to stop this one from controlling your thoughts and behavior, but by making yourself aware of these tendencies, you might be able to obtain more appointments and close more sales.

The next most powerful Driver is the "Try Hard".

Chapter 6
The Try Hard Driver

Main Characteristics:
- **You insist that you want to make a lot of money, but you feel unhappy or guilty when you do.**
- **People usually think of you as very self-confident, although you feel inferior.**
- **People say about you, "Poor Joe. He tries so hard but just can't seem to make it."**
- **You prefer sympathy instead of success, even though you will not admit it.**
- **When you do succeed in making a lot of money, your contracts are often cancelled and your commissions taken back, causing your manager, associates and family members to express sympathy.**
- **You work long hours to show your family that you are trying so hard to provide for their needs and wants, but you achieve very little in terms of income.**

Little Johnny was born into a family of a father who was a Gold Medalist in the Olympics for gymnastics, a mother who was Valedictorian at Harvard, an older brother who excelled in high school sports, and a sister who maintained a perfect 4.0 average. After bringing home several report cards of C's and D's and being advised not to try to be on the Little League team, his parents decided that Little Johnny would never amount to much. Attempting to be kind, they told him not to worry about schoolwork or sports, but just to try hard and they would love him. So he tried hard. Every time he tried and didn't do well, his parents gave him sympathy; and every time he tried and failed his parents and sister gave him more sympathy and pity. In his little mind, sympathy was "love", and all children want to be loved. Unlike his brother and sister who were shown off by his parents, Little Johnny felt no reason to value himself or his time. Worse still, the parents showed no interest in teaching him the value of self-discipline or a work ethic, and so he grew up fiddling away his time doing whatever he wanted. He was a friendly fellow and people liked him, but they didn't expect much from him. Every time he got a job and didn't do well, his parents and friends would be sympathetic, so at least he felt loved. He finally moved away from his parents and rented an apartment with a friend, but he had a hard time staying with the various jobs he tried. Finally, he had to move into somebody's rent-free basement while that landlord tried to help him get back on his feet. What upset Johnny the most about this person was that he didn't sympathize with Johnny's plight or pity him, thus Johnny didn't feel appreciated. One day this landlord brought a carload of pictures home from an estate sale. He told Johnny to carry a couple down to an office park and see if he could sell them. Anything over the $5.00 cost would be Johnny's profit. To his delight, Johnny sold both of them to a business owner who offered him $30 each before he had even opened his mouth to suggest a price. He ran home to brag, and the man gave him two more, which he promptly sold for $30 each. Soon all the pictures had been sold and Johnny counted his total income for the day--$240. Suddenly he felt sad. His need for being stroked as a "near-do-well" overrode an otherwise normally experienced feeling of pride in being successful.

In 1992, I developed my first Personality Assessment test, the predecessor of the present *One Assessment* that you will learn more about in Section III. One of its main functions was to identify the Try Hard Driver in sales candidates. In the companies that hired me to screen sales candidates, managers most generally took my advice in not hiring those who had exhibited the Driver, though sometimes they ignored my advice. In every case where the candidate had this Driver, two results occurred. Either the employee quit or got fired, or just barely hung on to that sales job, robbing the company of its ability to fill that position with a better producer. Like "drinking and driving", sales and the Try Hard Driver don't mix. Like the Caretaker and Pleaser Personality Drivers, the Try Hard Driver is tied to the survival mechanisms of the person. Love is a basic need just as is air and water.

We get weak and sick without love. Little Johnny became sad when he made $240 because he wanted the sympathy and pity that could have come had he failed at selling. Those with the Try Hard Driver do not get excited about the normal motivations of selling which include more money, winning contests and being able to afford the finer things in life. To the Try Hard, failing at selling is success, because the sales manager and other agents will give sympathy and pity—things experienced by the agent as love. Can you overcome this one by yourself? Maybe you could in 40 years. Do you want to struggle another 40 years or do you want to work with somebody who spent 40 years overcoming this Driver, who can teach you to overcome it in a few months?

Self-Help and How-To

While selling, you must become aware of your tendencies to….
- Spend an excessive amount of time in "busy-work" that prevents you from cold calling to set appointments.
- Give an excellent sales presentation to a prospective client, but say something that causes the person not to buy.
- Feel guilty when you set an appointment or make a sale
- Feel sad when you set an appointment or make a sale
- Feel no excitement in entering a sales contest
- Do anything that causes others to feel sorry for you

As with all drivers, you will not be able to stop the Try Hard from controlling your attitudes and behaviors, but you might set more appointments and close more sales by simply becoming aware of the characteristics listed above.

The next strongest adversary is the Withhold Driver.

Chapter 7

The Withhold Driver

Main Characteristics:
- **The classic example of this Driver is that the person got hired because the sales management believed that he might become a record-breaker.**
- **This is a person with all the potential in the world— good looks, a captivating presence, high energy, an infectious enthusiasm, intelligence, ability to talk to anybody about anything anytime-- but who produces little.**
- **It is the person the sales manager continues to watch, mystified as to how to unlock the personality or to motivate the agent into action.**

Every sales manager or real estate broker has watched a sales agent with the Withhold Driver, wondering what it will take to cause him or her to produce. The agent typically has all the potential in the world for selling but cannot make it work. Listening to his new agent's cold or lead calls the manager is convinced that this agent will be a winner, but is always disappointed by the few appointments made. Going with this agent on a sales appointment is also a big disappointment. Afterwards the sales manager might say, "I don't understand it, Bob. You make a better presentation than I do, but the customer still doesn't buy. I just don't understand it. Just call more people and see more and I'm sure you'll take off at any minute," but Bob never takes off. The problem is not in what he says or how he says it, but in what message he is sending subliminally—that is, unconsciously. The customer sees a well-dressed person and hears all the right words articulated just as have been taught by the best of salesperson models, but there is an undercurrent that confuses the client and therefore warns him not to trust or buy from this agent. It's as if Bob is saying with his lips, "Please buy", but with his heart is saying, "Please don't buy." What causes Bob to self-sabotage his sales? The answer--revenge.

Do you like revenge plots in movies and books? In your secret fantasies are you a sadist or a masochist? Do you feel hatred toward anybody? Do you hold grudges and have a difficult time forgiving others or yourself? You could be another Bob. Psychology statistics tell us from observations of the general population and scientific studies, that approximately one third of children under the age of 5 have been abused sexually, physically or emotionally. "Before age 5" is significant because the memory does not mature until then. Before age 5 you may have random memories here and there, but the memories of longer periods of time and events do not solidify until age 5 and after as a rule. This means that if you were abused in one of these three ways before age 5, you probably would not remember it, but would react to it for the rest of your life. Perhaps you read about people who committed heinous crimes only to learn from a family member years later that some form of torture was practiced on the perpetrator before age 5. The archives are jammed with stories of women who were sexually abused in the first 12 to 48 months of life and suffered with the symptoms all their lives thinking that they were demon possessed or mentally ill. What are the two main problems with being abused before age 5?

The First is that the child feels hatred toward the person who abuses him, but cannot express it. If the abuser is a parent or another adult who is responsible for the child's well-being, then the child is completely dependent on that adult. The child senses the danger and cannot express hatred toward the authority figure. As a result of needing to express that hatred, the child then turns it into self-hatred. What do you think self-hatred does to your self-identity, self-image, self-esteem and self-confidence? It sabotages all of those things. Children are thrust into many situations simply because they are trying to survive or make sense of self-hate. The situations are endless and all turn out badly because the self-identity and self-image always sees that self as dysfunctional and defective. How can you have hope and a positive feeling about yourself when you hate yourself? Do you see how self-hatred could affect your sales ability?

The Second problem is that when the child is no longer totally dependent, he will turn that self-hatred on other people. Other people do not include the parent as a rule, but rather are substitutes for the parent. Does this problem only occur in the lower classes? No, many are the cream of society, well educated with important jobs. Some are even ministers. Nobody escapes childhood unscathed. Are you one of these with the Withhold Driver? If so, you might well be a poor salesperson, maybe even one with all the potential that is self-sabotaging every sale above those required to meet your quota.

Self-hatred and hatred toward others is not caused only because of abuse before age 5. Being bullied when older than five, tortured, humiliated, feeling neglected, isolated, learning a prejudice or being subjected to many forms of violence can cause one to hate the self or others.

Isn't it amazing that childhood trauma plays such an important part of a salesperson's poor performance or failure? How many of your friends have washed out of sales jobs? The most painful thing that happens to a salesperson who has this Withhold Driver is what he does to his family. Let's say that he has a healthy marriage, loves his wife and three children and prays for their well being every night. He wants the best for them and he wants to be able to give significant sums of money to the church and charities, but he won't do a thing about it—not even for his own wife and children. He continues to sabotage every sale except the ones that meet his quota. He withholds his abilities so as to hate himself and others out there who he will never meet. He loves revenge. Think of it, he has the ability to sell a service that could help so many people but he withholds that service to hurt them, to get even with them for the abuse done to him. Is that crazy? He wonders and so does his manager, his spouse and children, his friends, everybody who sees what he is doing; yet he cannot stop his behavior. He is a Withhold machine. Do you have this Withhold Driver? If you do, you could spend the next 60 years overcoming it, or you could contact me and stop its effects within months. Do you really love your spouse, your children, and all those charitable causes you think you care about? Prove it. Contact me and let's stop the Withhold.

Lane A Stokes L.P.C.

Self-Help and How-To

When selling, be aware of your tendencies…
- To enjoy movies and books with revenge plots
- To hold grudges for a long time
- To refuse to forgive others for transgressions against you
- To sabotage all sales beyond those needed to meet your quota
- To deliver "perfect" sales presentations with an attitude of hoping to fail
- To feel sad when you see your family needing more money
- To feel sad when you have no money to give to church or charities

Now brace yourself for the next strongest Driver, the "I Don't Matter".

Chapter 8
The "I Don't Matter" Driver

Main Characteristics:
- **Achieves intermittent success**
- **Experiences mood swings with high achievement to low**
- **Thinks in terms of "black or white"**
- **Is the classic "flash in the pan" salesperson who out-sells everybody else in the beginning and then sells almost nothing.**
- **Wears a long face and depresses everybody around him**

Do you remember Little Johnny? He didn't have this Driver because he believed that he mattered to his parents, brother, sister, and everybody else. At least they gave him the sympathy and pity he misinterpreted for love. Even though he got thrown off the Little League team, his parents and siblings did attend every game. When he attempted to learn the clarinet his family attended his concerts. Johnny felt special and loved because his family attended all his events. Johnny mattered to himself and to his family. While it was true that he didn't value himself too highly in terms of work, he did manage to live apart from his parents all of his life by earning a basic wage.

Melanie was different. She didn't matter to anybody. It's remarkable that she didn't kill herself. Probably the only reason she didn't was because of her religious upbringing. A lonely child, she played with dolls for longer than most, moved the figures around her elaborate doll house her father had lovingly built for her, did her household chores without being told, ate her spinach, and baby sat for a few neighbors. Her grades were B's and A's, but she participated in no school clubs and went to church with her family every week unless sick or sleeping over with her one best friend. She was a good kid, a bother to nobody and she came and went as she pleased. Boys didn't call her because she was homely and stubbornly refused their advances. It wasn't that she was unfriendly; she just didn't seem interested in people in general or in their favorite activities. At age 16 her beautiful voice was discovered, and she was urged to join a school chorus. That got her interested in playing the piano, but none of her family attended her choral or piano performances. Her father was always too busy working and her mother seldom felt well enough to bother with such things. After graduating from high school she enrolled in a local college so she could save money by living at home. During the sophomore year when she was supposed to declare her major, she had no idea what to do and chose elementary school education. With no prospects of marriage, unlike many girls her age, she silently slipped into teaching little children 200 miles from her parent's home, and shared an apartment with two other teachers. For extra money she tried selling cosmetics door to door but did poorly. Then she got a job selling logo-marketing materials to local businesses. Having so little energy or interest in that job, she gave up the idea of extra spending money. She didn't need it anyhow. She had all she needed from her teaching job. During the summer she lay around reading books and watching children playing in a large park near her apartment. Are you bored yet? What might have she have become if her parents had treated her as somebody special? Anything!… the sky would have been the limit. What are the dynamics of the "I Don't Matter Driver"?

For one, she was a lonely child. She played with dolls for more years than most girls. The chief emotion of loneliness is sadness. The sidekicks of sadness are usually depression and discouragement. You read the story. It almost put you to sleep, didn't it? Her life was so blah, so bland, so boring, and so plain. There was no high energy here, no passion, and no interests outside of mere survival. Simply existing is not something that excites or inspires us. Would you want a life like hers? Do you have one like it now? Have you ever had a similar life? Well, you might be surprised how common her story is and how many people are looking for ways get out of this world because of the plainness of their existences. Some people escape by committing suicide, while others have turned to alcoholism, drug or sex addictions, and even technology addictions. I worked with troubled adolescent boys for a year in a wilderness setting. With nothing to do but watch the campfire burn, these young men talked openly about their histories. One common denominator for all of them was marijuana. They liked it because it took away their initiative to do anything else. In other words, they didn't feel guilty for doing nothing when they smoked at least one joint a day. Drugs will always have a place in our society for that one purpose—to zone out of life because living is too difficult. So, the first dynamic of the "I Don't Matter" Driver is having nothing much for which to live or not deserving to have anything.

A second dynamic of this "I Don't Matter Driver" was that Melanie's parents did not value her enough to discipline her to accomplish anything beyond her chosen activities. Maybe it was because she was not a bother to them, or maybe it was because she was just a girl who was supposed to grow older, get married and have a family. Her father was always working, so he must have understood his value. The mother was always resting or playing bridge with friends, no doubt fulfilling the role set for her by her generation and her family. Melanie had tried selling cosmetics door to door while teaching, to supplement her meager salary. What if, at age 15, her father had urged her to sell cosmetics in the neighborhood and used his business experience to inspire her to become really successful? How would he have done it? First, he could have talked to her about the nice clothes she could have bought with the extra money, or of the red sport's car she could have driven. After getting her excited and hopeful, he could have helped her schedule a couple hours every school day and all day Saturday to knock on doors and meet the ladies in the neighborhood, perhaps giving them a token gift in return for a short visit or a purchase. Every time Melanie could have chosen to play with her dolls instead of spending those hours knocking on doors, her father could have taken away a privilege, maybe a doll or two. Soon his disciplining her would have grown inside her as self-discipline. When she amassed nearly enough money for the car, her father could have taught her price-negotiation so that she could drive the car off the lot. Then she could have watched the heads turn as she drove by her friends. By the time she was ready to go to college, she might have been excited about applying herself to a business degree instead of just settling for teaching. Self-discipline is what saves us from boredom and wasted days and years. Self-discipline is needed badly to succeed in sales. If your parents did not discipline you, you probably have little self-discipline now.

A third dynamic, then, is to value yourself. Melanie could have given up selling because it was her father's idea. She could have failed at the business school in college to work in a homeless shelter or perhaps to end up living in one. In the final analysis the only true security is your ability to count on yourself to do what is needed to support those you love and yourself. This requires desire and this is the most lacking ingredient in 80% of salespersons. The 20% have more than their share. Ask a 20% personality what they want and they could write you a list three pages long. Ask an 80% personality and you would be lucky to get five things. What about you? Sit down and write across the top of the page "What I Want" and list them all. I'll bet that you cannot think of 30, maybe not 20, and maybe not even 10. Those who feel that they don't matter feel that they are not worthy of having what they want—only what they need. In sales you only need to meet your quota. Those with the "I Don't Matter Driver" seldom even meet that need and find themselves not working for that company very long. And you know what, "It doesn't matter" because that person doesn't matter and nothing matters because of his or her lack of self-worth. There's that old TV ad in which the woman is showing off an expensive dress and says, "Because I'm worth it!" She would do well in sales.

Self-Help and How-To

Become aware of your tendencies to...
- Feel bored and lazy
- Have no interests and no personal or business goals
- Feel worthless
- Stay with a schedule a very short length of time
- Not make all the cold or lead calls that you set as a goal
- Use marijuana or experiment with illegal drugs

Now we come to the worst of the worst, The "I Will Not" Driver.

Chapter 9
The "I Will Not" Driver

Main Characteristics:
- **Not getting out of bed upon awaking but staying there with arms and ankles tightly crossed.**
- **Beginning to make cold or lead calls by phone and then stopping abruptly.**
- **Going out on calls but sitting in the car rather than going in.**
- **Missing appointments.**
- **Continuing such irrational behavior while questioning one's sanity.**
- **States to self or others, "I will not" do something. (Can you now understand why the Driver is akin to a mental illness in the way it controls a person's mind and emotions?)**

At one point I considered this the same as the Withhold Driver until I learned how different they are. The "Withhold person" will work if only half-hearted. He may withhold because of revenge or hatred, but the force of the "Withhold Driver" is nowhere as powerful as the "I Will Not". This last one is the most powerful of all of the drivers included in this book, for controlling one's attitudes and behaviors. At least knowing that it is hatred and revenge that makes one withhold, provides some comfort and something to grab onto in overcoming it, but this is not so with the "I Will Not." There seems to be no reason as to what causes it.

Roger had been selling for an insurance company for 2 years. He exercised near perfect control over his daily schedule for 10 hours a day, five and one half days a week. His income was close to $100,000 a year. Everybody admired his skills of organization, his friendly and kind manners, and they invited him to all their parties and functions.

Using his electronic equipment, he mapped out all the businesses he was to visit by the month, so that every day was an easy movement from place to place. One day Roger parked in front of the next office building he was to enter, put his hand on the door handle and nothing happened. He didn't move. It wasn't that the door handle didn't work or he couldn't have gotten out of the car, he just didn't. Sitting there mystified by his behavior, he began talking to himself, questioning what was happening. Was he having a stroke? No. Was he having a nervous breakdown? He didn't think so. So why wasn't he getting out to call on Mr. Johnson on the fourth floor in suite 405? He didn't have a clue. For 20 minutes he sat there, wondering if he had lost his mind. Not wanting to go home lest his wife think it strange, he sat there another 20 minutes. Finally he drove to Starbucks and had a latte, staring into the abyss of his silence. He had never experienced anything like this. Calling his sales manager didn't seem wise, so he called a friend and got the voice mail. Feeling a little more desperate, he drove to a local mental health facility where he felt he could retain anonymity. He offered to pay full price for the privilege of seeing a psychiatrist. For 50 minutes they stared at each other. With no consolation or feedback of consequence, he drove home and told his wife what had happened. He felt bewildered and ashamed. The only thing he wanted to do was to hide his shame, so he went into the bedroom and lay down. He had never lain down in the middle of the day since he was a child. For 2 hours he lay with his arms and ankles crossed, locked, and repeated over and over, "I will not, I will not, I will not." Then he fell asleep and slept till 10:00 AM the next morning. He had not slept that late since high school. When he woke up, nothing had changed. He kept his arms and ankles locked and his eyes closed.

Outside of knowing how to "fix" this Driver, there is not much more to say about it. You can tell from this excerpt how terrifying and baffling Roger's experience was and how it would distress a normal person. You might also be interested to know how many people have this Driver. I was. Years ago one of my supervisors forced me to experience my own feelings of helplessness so that I could identify with my clients. Later I did it again—for 48 hours—it was like riding a raging bull, I would think, and it exhausted me. For every emotion, I put myself through the same ordeal. When I got to shame I ended up in the hospital. Emotions are very powerful, but nothing like the power of Unconscious Personality Traits and Drivers, especially Drivers.

Self-Help and How-To

Become aware of your tendencies…
- To stop working abruptly with the only reason as "I will not"
- To not to get out of bed in the morning
- To refuse to begin work on any day
- To feel that you are going crazy because you will not work
- To miss an appointment that you have set

Summary of Traits and Drivers

Personality Traits and Drivers are those unseen barriers that prompt 80% of the population to feel that something is holding them back from getting what they want. To finally be told what those barriers are is a great relief to most. Identifying the problem is half the battle. In some cases, simply recognizing the problem is enough to dismiss its power, but when the barrier persists it is time to call for assistance. These Traits and Drivers are most often beyond the expertise of sales managers and sales coaches. You should never consult motivational tapes and self-help books. You wouldn't read a book to learn how to extract an infected kidney. All Traits and Drivers as defined in this book have the same power as a mental illness, and understanding how mental illness controls personality components is a requirement for overcoming such barriers. Even if your sales manager or coach were a trained psychotherapist, it would be doubtful that he or she would be knowledgeable of the Traits and Drivers described in this book, because nowhere are they taught in school. They are the result of more than four decades of my own personal research and experience.

Keep in mind that the Traits and Drivers mentioned in this book are different from the forces to which such behaviors are most generally ascribed such as the Passive Aggressive, the Victim Martyr, the Approach/Avoidance and so forth. Most assessments and sales training are based on these classic psychological features and not upon my own research as expressed in my own terminology.

Now that we have explored the Traits and Drivers that cause the 80% to continue selling only 20% of goods and services, let's look at the solutions being used to change the 80% Personality to the 20%.

Section III
Successful Solutions For Sales Self-Sabotage

No matter what personality trait or driver prevents achievement, every one of them can be overcome or changed. Sometimes the individual can change a trait by simply seeing its effect. Very few drivers are changed by introspection, however, because the person is seldom that objective about the self. Drivers are best changed by professionals. The solutions in this section are very helpful to those intending to move toward 20% achievement levels because of the speed with which the solutions provide change. Take the *One Assessment*, for instance. It identifies every trait and driver preventing achievement that has been discovered thus far, and can begin to change those traits and drivers while the person is taking it.

The One Assessment

While still working with the patients in a mental health clinic diagnosed with the Borderline Personality Disorder, I was invited to speak to a Kiwanis Club in Atlanta about my study. One of the members invited me to help him hire salespeople. Knowing nothing about hiring, I wrote 100 questions to give me a "snapshot" of a person's personality structure, especially of those components that cause low achievement and failure. Asking those questions made it as easy as picking "bananas from apples" as to who would fail or would be the most successful in sales. After that, two other companies asked me to screen their sales candidates, and I also screened applicants for positions for management, accounting, and administration. I gained the reputation for being accurate 100% of the time in making the right fit and having the employee achieve that for which he was hired. Over the past 21 years

I have added many more questions and now have an assessment that deters falsification of responses.

It's funny how things turn out, isn't it? In 2010 I was asked to volunteer at my church in the Career Ministry for helping the unemployed find jobs. During that time I administered my *One Assessment* to aid in identifying the best attributes of a person, and I quickly discovered that more was needed to help the people get hired. With the help of those who completed the assessment, together we created a way of teaching them to exude all of their best qualities into a hiring interview, with remarkable results during a time when few were being hired. It was a "connection thing"-- more than simply knowing one's best characteristics--but actually connecting with people out there who wanted to hire them. My next clue was to come in 2012.

In 2012, I was fortunate to be invited to speak to the agents at a well-respected insurance company and as a result created a group seminar mode for doing some of what I had originally done in individual sessions. Putting on paper in an organized fashion what had only been in my head all my life caused me to understand more about how I was able to change my own personality in 1979, to so quickly "cure" the three Borderlines in 1992, and get jobs so quickly for the unemployed in 2010. It was what I called "prompting the unconscious mind". As a result, I re-wrote my *One Assessment.*

The One Assessment now has many advantages over other assessments on the market:

1. Simply completing the assessment due to my use of *Prompting the Unconscious Mind* begins the process of higher achievement.
2. Every important unconscious personality trait that causes low or high achievement is pinpointed.
3. Every question is indexed to a solution for overcoming self-sabotaging or low achievement traits or drivers.
4. Every high achievement trait is determined by visual and auditory observation and by the questions answered. In this way I can easily and accurately choose the upper 20% to 1% Personalities required for the highest paying jobs for companies.

5. Nobody can cheat on this assessment.
6. It is perfect for those wanting to know if a sales position is the work for them without wasting money and a lot of time finding out.
7. All the information can be used for management of the individual.
8. I use it to write a schedule of traits and drivers that I then systematically overcome or change to change the 80% personality into the 20% personality.
9. While everybody answers the same questions, there is no adding up numbers to place the person in a category for comparison to others. All responses are cross-referenced to describe only the personality of the person taking the assessment.

The One Assessment was responsible for allowing me to "Hire the Right Person the First Time" for companies, giving the 100% success rate.

The Mini-One Assessment

This 30-minute assessment was originally created to meet the needs of a business development firm in Oakland, California. This firm helps companies across the country in setting up sales staffs. Instead of flying candidates to Atlanta to take the *One Assessment*, the "Mini" can be administered over the telephone to determine suitability for sales. If the candidate were to pass the Mini, then the expense of the *One Assessment* could be more easily justified. The Mini, therefore, saves companies thousands of dollars by preventing those not suited for sales from being interviewed or hired.

There are many other uses for the Mini. Those thinking of becoming real estate agents can prevent the expenses of becoming licensed, buying new wardrobes and leasing expensive cars by finding out ahead of time if they are suited for selling. Others seeking to sell insurance or financial products can save the cost of licensing and lost time in training by taking the Mini to determine their suitability for selling. For those already in a sales career, the results of the Mini can help them know which areas of their personality need attention to increase sales. The abundance of personality assessments in schools and colleges may determine that those taking the test are generally suited for selling, but the Mini will tell them more precisely if their individual personalities will succeed.

Commission-only sales jobs have been created across America since 2008 to provide employment for those having lost their jobs. Approximately 85% of those recruited for these jobs normally wash out within the first twelve months, but during this time they take up space in the office and consume the time of trainers. While it is true that these companies may induce the salespersons to sell the services or products to their family and friends, the company could do better in the long run by having the Mini administered during the recruitment process. In this way, the company could fill their positions with more productive agents who would earn much more for the company than the little bit earned by non-productive agents who would sell only to those they know.

Re-Imaging

We all tend to live up to the image we have of ourselves. If we desire to be a better person, to do and have more, we then create a new image. This is what I learned to do when working with the three Borderlines in 1991. When I began that Borderline "experiment" or study, I had no roadmap to follow because nobody had ever done a similar study before. At that time, borderlines were considered hopeless as evidenced by the fact that no insurance company or government agency would reimburse professionals for their therapy. My reason for attempting the project in the first place was that I was not willing to believe that anybody was hopeless. A few years before, in my internship at a geriatric hospital, four of us worked with a psychopath deemed hopeless by the psychiatrists. We helped him live a normal life of work in his own home. I believed that I could do something similar for Borderlines. I had no idea that what I was about to undertake would "cure" them by giving them a new image or rather, the first real Self they had ever had. One of the key, defining characteristics of the Borderline Personality Disorder is the absence of a Self. What distinguishes Re-Imaging from the popular DBT of today is that Re-Imaging produces a permanent Self while DBT seems to remain effective as long as the Borderline remembers to repeat the suggested phrases and performs the required meditation. Once my patients developed a Self they also had the possibility of having self-esteem, self-confidence, self-image, and anything else pertaining to the Self. They began building the self-esteem and self-confidence so necessary to carry them through life as autonomous individuals no longer totally dependent on the mother.

I use Re-Imaging for salespeople in the same way I learned to do it for the Borderlines. It is perhaps the most powerful tool for changing the personality of the 80% group to that of the 20% group because it reassigns new images for all the personality drivers and traits. This is accomplished by using imagery totally unrelated to the way the mind usually conceptualizes reaching a goal. Re-Imaging allows my clients to reach seemingly impossible goals in relatively short spans of time. It reassigns new images all at the same time through a process I call "Prompting the Unconscious Mind."

Prompting the Unconscious Mind

If you have never heard this term, it is because it is another one of my own ways of describing my own conceptualizations of what I see happening. One lady heard me talking about it and said, " Oh, I understand. You are using hypnosis and guided self-imagery." I corrected her by saying that I have NOTHING to do with hypnosis or self-guided imagery. *Prompting the Unconscious Mind* for purposes of changing the 80% to the 20% personality begins by allowing the person to see the adverse effects of a particular trait or driver. Then the person is shown how to identify which trait or driver it is and how his life would be different without it. Next, the person is shown a way to overcome, neutralize or eliminate that trait or driver. This can be done verbally or visually. Again, the speed of overcoming the personality barriers that retain a personality in the 80% category comes from the fact that in one meeting a salesperson can view ten or more unconscious traits or drivers and command the unconscious mind to begin overcoming them all at the same time. While the conscious mind can focus on only one trait at a time, the unconscious mind can focus on a hundred or more. Have you ever seen "plate spinning" at a circus or on a talent show? A person spins what looks like a dinner plate on top of a stick about 5 feet high and then another and another until 20 plates are spinning. As the first one loses momentum and begins to wobble, the person runs back and spins it again, and then the next and the next. This is how the unconscious mind overcomes so many traits at the same time. A "cue" provided keeps the "plates" spinning until the traits are overcome. It takes a lifetime to create the hundreds of personality traits that define the 80%, and by all rights it should take four or five lifetimes to neutralize their power by the conscious mind. Do you see now how it is possible to change the 80% Personality to the 20% within 12 months are less? By itself, *Prompting the Unconscious Mind* stops multiple barriers from controlling the salesperson. By using Re-Imaging in addition to "Prompting", the time period would be less.

Individual Sessions

Individual and group sessions every week are the fastest way to change the 80% Personality to the 20%. For those who can only afford the individual sessions, the *One Assessment* is used to pinpoint every significant driver and trait, a plan is devised in descending order from most to least important, and every week we work through those issues until the salesperson is selling at the upper 20% level of achievement. The two advantages of the individual sessions are being able to focus on the traits of the individual and the privacy of talking about sensitive experiences one would never speak of in a group. Role-play for telephone calling to verify authenticity and connection can be more immediate. The chief drawback that the individual session has is the lack of synergy only a group can produce.

Group Sessions

The group produces Synergy, a phenomenon sometimes called "change on steroids". Talk about spinning 100 plates by the unconscious mind! The group is the best way to get those traits spinning (being processed) at a tremendous momentum with continuous cues. Groups are fun, and by two doing one role-play, everybody else identifies with and learns at the same time. Many private matters can be handled in group role-play and group sharing. Old emotions, patterns of emotions, and attachments can be eliminated by group synergy. The drawback of the group or seminar approach is that subjects covered are more general and do not follow a plan of action as with the individual. This is why combining the individual and group approaches are so important. Instead of spending a lot of time in individual sessions learning how to use the telephone or how to listen, the group process is perfect, as each member learns a lot by listening and observation of others. Weekly follow-up on what agents said and what results were achieved in a group is invaluable because the sharing of what was and was not effective spurs all the members to improve for the next week.

You can use what you have learned in this book by forming your own group of sales agents. The first exercise you should perform is the Authenticity Test. Have each member read these three sentences to the others: 1)" I care about you and want to help you. 2) I just want money. 3) I hate selling. I just want money". After each member reads the three sentences, the group votes on which sounded the most authentic. If a salesperson reads all three and is told that #3 sounds the most authentic, then the group needs to discuss with him what his real motive is for selling. We think that we should say that we sell because we care about our clients and want to help them. But if the agent tells his client that he cares about him and the client senses that the agent really hates selling and just wants money, then the client may sense the lack of authenticity, and refuse to buy. As a group, you get the person to be honest about his or her motives. It is fine if the salesperson sells just to make money and does not care emotionally for the client, because the act of selling what the client needs is an act of caring. Once the salesperson becomes clear what his real motive is, have him read the three sentences again. In one such seminar group, a salesperson tripled the number of appointments for the next week after discovering just one simple motive.

Neuroscience and Cues

Neuroscience is a big buzzword in 2013 and the using of "cues" to overcome constraining behaviors is popular as well. Keep in mind that the uses of the term "neuroscience" in this book are not about the sophisticated lab experiments conducted by doctors. The uses for this book have to do with "cues" that cause the unconscious mind to overcome more than one personality trait at a time. When I first heard the term "neuroscience" this year and read a little about it, I became excited, thinking that this would be a new addition to my research. But the more I read, the more I realized that I had been using neuroscience and cues for decades. Much of Re-Imaging and Prompting the Unconscious Mind is accomplished by using cues. If you are not familiar with the term, it means using a common experience to remind the brain to change a belief or behavior whether consciously thinking about it or not. One of my cues, for instance, for Prompting the Unconscious Mind to keep the plates spinning, is washing one's hands. I tell my clients that every time they wash their hands they are sending a message to the unconscious mind to continue overcoming all the "negative" drivers and traits discovered so far. One client told me that he now washes his hands at every opportunity and longer than ever before. By using this as a cue, I am also promoting a healthier lifestyle. While I will learn all I can from what is being shared by the neuroscience enthusiasts, my passion will be re-ignited more when the modern buzzwords focus on "Thought Reception" and "Thought Transmission", something else I've been using for many decades.

The Power of Repetition

The power of repetition dates back at least to the ancient Hindus in 1000 BC and again in 500BC with the ancient Buddhists. I first learned about these ancient methods of repetitive prayers in theology school when I was trying to understand the meaning of "belief". My chief interest in these ancient prayers was how they produced the ability to believe. As any professional salesperson will assure you, believing is a big part of sales success. Believing in yourself, believing in the process of selling, and believing that the client will buy from you are all important parts of selling. When we repeat something that we want to believe will happen, the mere repetition usually, eventually, can cause us to believe that it is possible. Beyond believing that it is possible, some salespeople attest that their experience of continued repetition will actually cause them to get whatever they seek. Try it for yourself. Do you want to make a sale every day this week? Repeat "I am closing a sale every day this week" and see if it works. The ancients said that you will either get what you repeated or you will get to recognize whatever barrier is preventing you from having it. In modern terms, you will recognize which personality traits and drivers are preventing you from getting what you want. Then we use the methods provided for overcoming those barriers.

Summary of Successful Solutions

Every day I am seeking to discover new understandings of why people act as they do and to learn ways to guide them toward a more fulfilling life. For this reason the solutions of today will only be part of the solutions of tomorrow.

Lane A Stokes L.P.C.

SUMMARY OF SALES SELF-SABOTAGE

The Sales Paradigm is changing. The 20/80 distinction is fading into extinction as the Traits and Drivers of low achievers are being transformed into new personalities of high achievement. Companies no longer must waste millions on re-hiring but may instead retain all their sales agents, having them turned into top producers, gaining larger market shares and towering over their competitors. There is no longer a mystery as to how to get what one wants. It is no longer about "hocus pocus" but simply about science. You identify the unconscious personality traits and drivers holding you back and change them—or have them changed—to get whatever you want. If you are a mediocre or average salesperson now, you can become a top achiever.

Contact lanestokes18@yahoo.com to become the next person or company to be transformed. If you live outside Atlanta, GA, and wish to work with us in overcoming your traits and drivers, we can arrange other venues. Learn more about Lane Stokes on Linked In and websites provided.

Related Reading

Adler, Alfred. *Understanding Human Nature*. Translated by Colin Brett, Hazelden Foundation, Minnesota, 1927.

Bach, Richard. *Jonathan Livingston Seagull*. The Macmillan Publishing Co., New York, 1973.

Baird, Robert M. and Stuart E. Rosenbaum. *Hatred, Bigotry, and Prejudice*. Prometheus Books, New York, 1999.

Braiker, Harriet B. *The Disease to Please*. McGraw-Hill, New York, 2001.

Bodine, Echo. *A Still, Small Voice*. New World Library, California, 2001.

Bultmann, Rudolf. *New Testament and Mythology*. Fortress Press, Philadelphia, 1989.

Byrne, Rhonda. *The Secret*. DVD. TM 2006 TS Production LLC. 2006.

Goleman, Daniel. *Emotional Intelligence*. Bantam Books, New York, 1995.

Easwaran, Eknath. *The Dhammapada*. Nilgiri Press, California, 1985.

Embry, Ainslie Thomas and deBary, Theodore. *Hindu Tradition*. Mass Market Press, New York, 1972.

Encyclopedia Britannica. *Great Books, Plato, Augustine*, Encyclopedia Britannica, Inc., 1980.

Fromm, Erich. *The Art of Loving*. Perennial Library, New York, 1956.

Gladwell, Malcolm. *Blink*. Back Bay Books, New York, 2005.

Hall, Calvin S. *A Primer of Freudian Psychology*. New American Library, New York, 1979.

Hall, Calvin S. and Nordby, Vernon J. *A Primer of Jungian Psychology*. New American Library, NewYork, 1973.

Heidegger, Martin. *Being and Time*. Blackwell Publisher, Massachusetts, 1962.

Hicks, Zoe M. *Dream Catcher*. Prayer Point Press, Indiana, 2005.

- Gospel of Thomas
- The Holy Bible

Lane A Stokes L.P.C.

Horney, Karen. *Feminine Psychology.* W.W. Norton & Co., New York, 1967.

Jamison, Kay Redfield. *An Unquiet Mind.* Vintage Books, New York, 1995.

Kassinove, Howard and Tafrate, Raymond Chip. *Anger Management.* Impact Publishers, Inc., California, 2002.

Kopp, Sheldon. *An End to Innocence.* Bantam Books, New York, 1978.

Kushner, Harold. *Who Needs God.* Pocket Books, New York, 1989.

Masterson, James F. *The Narcissistic and Borderline Disorders.* Brunner/Mazel Publishers, New York, 1981.

Masterson, James F. *Psychotherapy of the Borderline Adult.* Brunner/Mazel Publishers, New York, 1976.

Masterson, James F. *The Search for the Real Self.* The Free Press, New York, 1988.

Maltz, Maxwell. *Psycho-Cybernetics.* Pocket Books, New York, 1960.

May, Rollo. *The Meaning of Anxiety.* Washington Square Press, New York, 1977.

Miller, Alice. *The Drama of the Gifted Child.* Basic Books, Inc., New York, 1981.

Miller, Jean Baker. *Toward a New Psychology of Women.* Beacon Press, Boston, 1976.

Nouwen, Henri J.M. *The Wounded Healer.* Image Books, New York, 1972.

Potter-Efron, Ronald and Patricia. *Letting Go of Shame.* HarperCollins, New York, 1989.

Sacks, Oliver. *Migraine.* Vintage Books, New York, 1992.

Siegel, Bernie S. *Love, Medicine & Miracles.* Quill, New York, 1998.

Spong, John Shelby. *Rescuing the Bible from Fundamentalists.* HarperSanFrancisco, New York, 1992.

Thompson, Clara M. *On Women.* New American Library, New York, 1986.

Tillich, Paul. *The Courage to Be.* Vail-Ballou Press, Inc., New York, 1952.

Tillich, Paul *The New Being.* Charles Scribner's Sons, New York, 1955.

Tillich, Paul. *The Shaking of the Foundations.* Charles Scribner's Sons, New York, 1948.